Quick, fetch me a pen, I need to write this down.

Emma Poore

Presentation by *BookLeaf Publishing*

Web: www.bookleafpub.com

E-mail: info@bookleafpub.com

ISBN : 9789357448222

First edition 2021

DEDICATION

Mum, Dad, Natalie, Sarah, Jamie, Lea, Charlie, Bethany, Charlotte and Bethan. Thank you for everything, you're all amazing and I'm very lucky to have you in my life.

ACKNOWLEDGEMENT

A big thank you to the creators of this writing challenge for re-connecting me with writing and helping me to re-discover my love for poetry. Thank you to the people who have inspired me and have made me who I am.

PREFACE

This book is filled with my poetic musings at various points throughout my life. I don't like forcing poetry, so I tend to write them in one sitting, like connecting a pen to my thoughts. This book includes poems about people of significance to me and experiences which have been of great impact in my life.
I am a big fan of William Blake and as with his works, you may see the influence of my identity as a Christian in some of my poems. My family values also strongly impact on my writing as you will be able to notice. I have also written poems based on my experiences working with the older generation within my job in older adult mental health.

The Weeping Tree

I fall with beauty, I fall with grace,
the image of my father's face.
I nimbly dance among the trees,
with fragile steps upon the breeze.

But when the winter comes I see,
there is no longer room for me.
The trees, they shiver, they feel the cold.
What happened to their cloaks of gold?

It hurt his heart to see you fall,
another lost, deaf to his call.
You are now dull, no longer bright.
Now all is dark, where once was light.

The trees look barren, again they shed,
an amber tear which leaves you dead.
Slipping, sliding, falling, fear.
Where is my master whom I call dear?

But in the embers of his pain,
a flame ignites with hope again.
He sends the world his most beloved,
a baby boy, a prince, a dove.

Did he who made the lamb make thee?
The one who saved all sinners, he
who freed us from captivity.
Who gives Love. Life. Eternity?

The spring returns in all its glory.
New blossoms, new life, a brand new story.
There's a chance once more for humankind,
depending on which path we find.

I fall with beauty, I fall with grace,
the image of my father's face.
But now I fall, the world to see,
that he who made the lamb, made me.

Grief

Rage, rage against the night,
there are some battles you have to fight.
It isn't fair, it isn't right,
when all seemed good, when all seemed bright.

But in your pain you understand,
a greater love, a greater plan.
Then when you're guided by that hand,
you really truly understand.

About his grace, about his love,
of all his blessings from above.
You don't think of loss,
but all you've gained.
Accept that and you'll find you've changed.

The world no longer bleak and cold,
a beating heart, a life to mould.
A comfort in your times of woe,
a greater strength, than most would know,
a place of shelter from your foe,
a resting place in which to go.

So should I fear, fret or cry,
should a tear fall from my eye,

I'll remember what I'm living for,
and of he I do adore.
Lonely I will never be,
if I'm with him and he's with me.

A Covid Scribble

A breeze blows down the avenue and I'm
thankful to be alive.
In a time that's filled with doubt and fear, I'm
glad that hope survives.

We need now, more than ever, to cling onto our
faith,
to know that love and joy remain and that they'll
keep us safe.

I look out on the horizon, the grassy banks and
sunny sky,
these beautiful surroundings, that I've been
passing by.

Is this what he's trying to teach us? A concept in
itself profound.
That whilst beauty lies around us, we've been
staring at the ground.

We ruminate on sad thoughts, fixate on the
unchanging.
Ignorant of all our blessings, our mind and soul
estranging.

How often in these last few months have we
talked just to talk,
been kind to others, walked just to walk?

Have we made time for all the people we're too
busy to usually see?
Can we just live inside the moment and laugh
because we're happy?

So switch of your phone and take off your shoes
and feel the earth beneath your feet.
Lie down in the grass and stare up at the sky, let
yourself feel complete.

Enjoy the warmth of the sun on your face and
listen to the bluebirds sing.
God's reminding you what matters, are you
listening?

The Significance of being Significant

When did it happen I wonder?
That point in time when I became insignificant?
Was it 40? 50? 60? I don't know.
Regardless, it happened didn't it?
My little birds grew up and flew off to their own
branches..
I'm immensely proud, don't confuse me as bitter.
Just lonely.

Of course, like dominoes, slowly one thing after
another happened.
Suddenly it was time to retire and take life at a
different pace.
Harry and I loved our "Golden years" as we
called them, for they truly were.
But all things must come to an end,
and now it's just me.
My children visit me of course, but they don't
live locally and they have their own families to
nurture.
Like I used to.

So here I sit,
the old lady in the corner.
You may not have noticed me, but I'm here.
Fighting to stay in the home that I love,
where I feel safe, and where so much love and
life happened.
Oh, so much life.

There are two types of people, I've found.
The people who want to make all my decisions,
to tie my life up with a neat little ribbon.
Then there's the people who see me, the real me.
I can tell how much they care about me, about
what I think and feel.
They make me feel SIGNIFICANT.
I had forgotten that feeling.

So, on behalf of people like myself, who might
have lost their voice.
Please don't forget about us.
We were you once. We had hopes and dreams of
our own.

So if you see us, don't just pass us by.
Sit, and talk a while.
Help us to feel significant again.

Midnight Musings

In the stillness I find peace,
in the beautiful moments of life,
where unrest quietens and chatter subsides.

And suddenly it's as if I'm soaring above the
clouds,
looking down at mountains and valleys below.
Ah, true serenity.

I love the night.
Not in some dark way,
I just love staring out the window at the brilliant
gleams of the moon, what are her secrets, do you
think she'll tell?
The twinkling splendour of the stars too, what
ancient knowledge do they hold?

The cool breeze caresses my skin, and it's
comforting, like a soft embrace.
I want to twirl around in that moonlight in my
bare feet, with my hair flowing around me.

I'll see you again tomorrow night, oh you
beautiful companions.

When I once again greet you in those far away
dreams that I so love to have. Where magic
exists.
Sleep tight, and for tonight, farewell.

Growth

You watch them growing up before your eyes,
learning from every mistake.
Getting back up whenever something knocks
them down,
and you don't realise, that they don't have all of
the answers either.

Your parents.
It's not until you're an adult too,
that you understand how much pressure they
must have felt,
but never let on.

They just kept turning up for you,
and being your hero again and again.

And if they've done their job,
then they will have prepared you for the big,
wide world.
And maybe at first, you'll ask
"What would Mum do?" or "What would Dad
do?"
But eventually, you will ask yourself
"What would I do?"

Whether they are still with us or not,
our parents can live on through us.
A little piece of them in the way we smile,
a gleam in our eye or a turn of phrase.

I would ask you,
is there a greater privilege?

Lindamore Marjorie May Poore

She sits there quietly smiling as she listens to the sound,
right here is where she's happy, with her family all around.
Not caught up with fancy baubles, a cup of tea she'd prefer,
for her family are her treasures, they're what matter most to her.

Well first place is already taken, for she loves and trusts in God,
she is leading by example, in the footsteps others trod.

She is called so many names, Nanna, Ma and Aunty Ma.
She is always on the phone, ringing friends from near and far.
She is valued oh so much, yet stays humble through and through.
She has many words of wisdom, but such wit and humour too.

I was 12 when I last saw you, the last time we
said goodbye,
there's so much I want to tell you, to sit and talk
whilst hours fly.
Your memory lives on in us, and we hope in us
you'd see,
that we are your living legacy, and evermore will
be.

Gerald Glyn

There is beauty in the small, everyday moments.
When a person shows how extraordinary they
are.
Not for thanks or for praise,
but because they simply must be that person.

My grandfather was one of these extraordinary
people.
In the light of sorrow and grief,
he rose above his pain and showed his strength.
His versatility, his heart and spirit.

Such is a man, that carries the labours of the
world on his back,
that doesn't make complaint or fuss,
but just quietly carries on working,
until the work is done.

I see him in my mother,
in her quiet and resilient strength.
Their love for us shines ever on,
guiding the way ahead,
keeping us from despair.

I promise to keep that light shining in me,

I promise to be as strong as I can.
And to quietly work on,
until the work is done.

Unconditional

Love without conditions,
impossible some would claim.
To be yourself completely,
free of guilt and free of shame.

Someone who loves you for you, and not the
person you "should" be.
Someone who truly gets you, and loves your
eccentricity.
Someone whose genius, wit and talent are just a
part of why they're great.
Whose also kind and thoughtful, with a laugh
that's just first rate.

And if we are together, then there's nothing we
can't achieve.
I've learned to be a cynic, but they'd help me to
believe.
That I deserve real love, not the shadow that I've
known,
in all these years of solitude, I've finally come
into my own.

My little imperfections, might make me perfect
in your view,

and despite my own self-doubts, I wouldn't have
to change myself for you.

So, unconditional is the word I choose, because
it really is so true,
my love has no conditions, so can I ask the same
of you?

Funny Girl

It's funny.
The definition of madness is doing the same
thing over and over.
Yet here I am at 25,
counting on my hands the amount of times that
this has happened to me.

The girl that doesn't get picked.
Some days it's easier to cope with,
but sometimes it hurts just as much as it did for
the first time at 16.

I guess I was always waiting for that to change,
to not let it define me.
But for better or worse, it's a part of me now.

The former dreams I had for myself were wisps
of things,
they pale greatly in comparison to the real joys
and blessings that my life has brought me.

And if I'm lucky, I'll get to see even more yet.

I could never have dreamed that my many
heartaches would bring me here.

But here I am anyway, bruised and battered,
but still standing.

And I'm stronger than I ever realised that I could
be.

I did this all on my own.
I built castles out of the rubble,
and I made the dull parts of my life shine
gloriously.

I'm on my own, but I'm not alone.

So, crushing disappointments may come,
and at first they can knock us down.
They can punch us in the gut,
and make us weep with sorrow.

Oh dark is that night.

But I take solace in remembering,
that a new dawn will break,
and the sun will come shining in,
and I'll remember that my heart doesn't need
mending,
because it was whole to begin with.

I Am Who I Am

I feel peaceful.
Calm in myself, restful.
I didn't chase this feeling and maybe that's why
it came to me.

True happiness comes from within us.
If we spend our lives chasing a feeling, chasing
a dream,
then we forget to stop and smell the roses,
we take everything we have for granted.

In fifty years will I remember the times that I
stayed late at work?
Or will I remember spending time with my
family and friends?
I know the answer.

So after years of searching for who I am and for
my place in this world,
I'm finally setting down roots.

I am who I have always been,
and who I am has always been enough.
But now I can finally see it.

Sisters

That magical land of childhood,
running around in the middle of the Triwizard
Tournment,
happily listening to "Concerning Hobbits".
It never feels better than when you were a child
does it?
With all of that youthful wonder and dreaming.

My sisters are my portal to that world,
they remind me to be my authentic self.
Sometimes kindly,
and sometimes in the language that only sisters
can use.
Of course with the caveat that no one else can
ever address you like that.

They are your girls,
your wingwomen throughout life.
They'll correct you when you're wrong,
but they're also the first people to lift you up
when life pushes you down.

They won't leave you lying there on the ground.
Let the world try and interfere with the love of a
sister, just you dare.

We aren't in the same city like we used to be,
but our hearts are never far from reach.
All it takes is a call, and they're there.

Because,
we're in this together.
Forever.

And I can't think of anyone I'd rather have by
my side.

My Extra Parents

They say it takes a village,
So why shouldn't this apply to us?
We were raised by a team.
The strong hands of my parents, grandparents,
uncles and aunts,
shaped us into the people we are today and lifted
us up.

We were luckier than most,
we had the privilege of being loved by so many.
They made sure that we had good manners and
taught us about respect.
They were also the first people to love us
unconditionally,
to remind us that this was no less than we
deserved.

So I'm thankful for my village,
for their love for me,
and for their belief in me when the going got
tough.

I am who you helped me to become.
And I hope you're proud of the beautiful things
in us,

that grew from the seeds you planted.

My Family

Dad's funny, wise and he's smart too.
Mum's practical, kind and always knows what to
say to you.
Full of advice and full of wit,
they're like chalk and cheese, but a perfect fit.

They're great as individuals, but stronger
together,
for they grew as a pair, when they promised
forever.
They had three children who knew they were
loved, who knew that they cared.
They fostered and encouraged, no cheerleader
compared.

This just the start of their little family,
with Emma and Sarah and of course, Natalie.
Now there's Lea and Charlie, the cutest kids
around,
and Jamie, the brother I love, though he's
sometimes a clown.

He treats my sister with love and dedication,
he works hard for his family, husband and father
are his true occupation.

These people I love, are what my heart holds
dear,
they take away my sadness, they take away my
fear.
So I'll pull them much closer, and say I love you
much more,
this is our family, the family of Poore.

Beauty

There's so much beauty in the world,
everywhere you go.
Beautiful things, beautiful people that you know.

Beautiful music, beautiful art,
drink them in, just start.
Listen with kindness and speak from the heart.

Don't hold onto feelings that will only drag you
down.
Make the choice to smile, instead of only frown.

When people compliment you,
don't stammer or stress.
Be glad for their words,
and that you managed to impress.

I believe that there is good in people,
it's in there, you'll see.
I know there's beauty in you,
and there's beauty in me.

And if we can simply feed it,
like a plant needs the sun,
then the dark clouds won't conquer,

for you'll have already won.

45

Sing

I love to sing, to fill up my lungs and really belt
it out.
To let go of my troubles, throw away my cares,
with a whisper, with a shout.

Singing can renew you,
it can make you feel at peace.
It can help you if you're hurting,
slowly mend you, piece by piece.

It can really make you happy,
laugh out loud, and dance with glee.
In a choir, duet or solo,
music makes great company.

So sing out with all your might,
until the air feels simply enchanted.
We're so lucky to have music,
so let's not take this gift for granted.

Purpose

I was always looking for my place in life,
for a real sense of purpose.
I wanted to help others,
to work for the National Health Service.

It took some time,
but in the end, I found the job for me.
My calling and my passion,
Occupational Therapy.

I get to help people,
to preserve their quality of life,
to help them overcome their struggles,
to overcome their strife.

I consider it a great honour,
to work with over 65s,
and I love to sit and listen,
whilst they talk about their lives.

I hope I can make a difference,
with my purpose, with my part.
And be a force for goodness,
giving care, that's from the heart.

Bethany

Our best friends are the family we choose,
or so people often say.
So, pick someone who gets you,
whose willing to stay.

They're there for our worst days, they're there
for our best.
They listen and counsel, put our worries to rest.

Everyone needs a best friend, I lucked out on
that front.
She's funny and badass, and also quite blunt.

We met at 11, our first day at high school.
Back when Twilight and flip phones and big
quiffs were cool.
I slowly approached her, I wanted a friend,
someone I could trust in, on whom to depend.

To tell her my secrets, my hopes and my dreams.
Someone to have jokes with, someone to share
memes.
I'll always defend her, she deserves to be happy,
she'll be shocked when she reads this, I'm not
usually this sappy.

She's more than I could've imagined,
in support I never lack.
She's always there to boost me,
she's always got my back.

She and I have been a duo now, for the last
fourteen years,
We've shared many laughs and we've shared
many tears.
Who knew back then, that we would be friends
for forever?
Everyone needs a Bethany, especially an Emma.

My Sisters from another Mister.. and Missus.

We've all been together,
for what feels like forever.
We grow and we change,
but our bond stays the same.

We played as children.
We hung out as adolescents.
We make time as adults,
swapping stories and presents.

We're not close in distance,
but still manage to speak.
Even Covid couldn't stop us,
with a new quiz every week.

We are quite the bunch,
and we each have our strengths.
Though we did learn the hard way,
it's not putting up tents.

Natalie is sassy, her humour couldn't be dryer.
We thought she was bragging, when she said
"I'm on fire!".
She's secretly sweet and people's opinion of her
matters,
If someone hurts her, her heart quietly shatters.
She's also quite bossy, she likes being a leader,
Meanwhile Sarah and I compete on whose
weirder.
We laugh at pure nonsense, Princess Clip Clop
delights her.
It's fun to imagine a cat at a typewriter.

Sarah is smart, she doesn't give herself enough
credit,
Ask her about a book, she's probably read it.
She's creative, she raps, she's a jack of all
trades!
You want personality? She's got it in spades.
She's ferocious at laser tag, she gets the job done
"Well, well, well, if it isn't Lonsdale London".

Bethan suits being a teacher, because she also
likes to lead
She makes detailed itineraries, and often likes to
read.
She's truly a Potterhead, there's not one fact she
doesn't know,

she's got plenty of style, but remember "Goats?
No".

Now Charlotte is sweet, she shapes children
every day.
She can't half make us laugh, and always knows
what to say.
She's patient and loyal, she knows how to
achieve,
she's stronger than she realises, if she'd only
believe.
She very sophisticated, she dresses well
consistently
"I must admit last night, I slept very gingerly".

I guess that leaves me, I'm quite often the
narrator,
I love to observe and write it down later.
My friends tell me I'm witty, that my humour is
strange,
but somehow I know, they don't want me to
change.
I'm not unintelligent, but I do have a ditsy side.
"Look at her, it must be chucking it down
outside".

There's a reason we're friends, even when life
gets messy,

and I'm glad for that October, when we first
became Bestie.

Little Lights of my Life

The day that I met you, I instantly knew,
that there would be nothing, I wouldn't do for
you.
So precious and small, you took over my world,
words can't describe how I love you dear girl.

It wasn't long after, that I met you, darling boy.
Your face has such sweetness, you express so
much joy.
Then came 2020, we spent a long time apart,
though I couldn't come to see you, you were
there in my heart.

You both have your characters, please always be
who you are.
She's feisty and funny, you've got an obsession
with cars.
Of all of my roles, I love Aunty with all my
might.
So keep shining brightly, little lights of my life.

Home

I found my own fortress in 2021,
I love that a new chapter has already begun.
Dad just retired, so that's excellent timing,
he paints and he drills, there's always new jobs
that he's finding.

So Dad is the handyman,
Mum's the royal paperor.
I'm the interior designer,
Nats is the expert decorator.

Together we've found that we make quite a
team,
we've tirelessly worked until the place seems to
gleam.
There's a comfort in knowing that my family is
near,
but this place feels like home, so I don't need to
fear.

I know Mum and Dad's house will always be my
home,
I know I can visit, or I can call on the phone.
But it's rather exciting, knowing this place is all
mine.

That I can love it and dress it, in colours
sublime.

After all of my saving for the house that I
bought,
I finally did it, and on my own who'd have
thought?
Please don't that think I'm bragging, I'm just
grateful and a little proud,
I didn't know if I could do it, but I never buckled
or bowed.

The house isn't big, but the walls are elastic,
there are nice things inside, even if the plates are
all plastic.
So on this, my last poem, I'll say with a grin.
This new chapters' just started, so let the fun
begin!